The Phoenix Living Poets

———————

RANSOMS

RANSOMS

by

LESLIE NORRIS

CHATTO AND WINDUS

THE HOGARTH PRESS

1970

Published by
Chatto & Windus Ltd
with The Hogarth Press Ltd
42 William IV Street
London WC2

★

Clarke, Irwin & Co Ltd
Toronto

SBN 7011 1595 5

Printed in Great Britain by
William Lewis (Printers) Ltd Cardiff

ACKNOWLEDGEMENTS

Many of these poems first appeared in *Akros*, *The Atlantic Monthly*, *The New York Times*, *Poetry Wales*, *The Anglo-Welsh Review*, *Priapus*, *Welsh Voices*, *The Sunday Telegraph* and *The Poet* (India). A number of them were included in the BBC Third Programme broadcasts, *Poetry Now*. 'A True Death' was previously published in *Vernon Watkins* (Faber and Faber), a memorial volume for the distinguished Welsh poet.

The generosity of The Welsh Arts Council gave me leisure to write some of the poems in this collection.

Contents

Cardigan Bay

(for Kitty)

The buzzard hung crossed
On the air and we came
Down from the hills under
Him. First sun from
The underworld turned
White his stretched surfaces,
Whitened the cracked stone

On this beach where end
The works of the sea,
The total husbandry
Of water. Now at noon
We walk the land between
The seamarks, knowing

That wave already made
To wash away our happy
Loitering before
We turn back into evening
Among the frail daffodils
Growing in other seasons.

For those who live here
After our daylight, I
Could wish us to look
Out of the darkness
We have become, teaching
Them happiness, a true love.

Water

On hot summer mornings my aunt set glasses
On a low wall outside the farmhouse,
With some jugs of cold water.
I would sit in the dark hall, or
      Behind the dairy window,
Waiting for children to come from the town.

They came in small groups, serious, steady,
And I could see them, black in the heat,
Long before they turned in at our gate
To march up the soft, dirt road.
      They would stand by the wall,
Drinking water with an engrossed thirst. The dog

Did not bother them, knowing them responsible
Travellers. They held in quiet hands their bags
Of jam sandwiches, and bottles of yellow fizz.
Sometimes they waved a gratitude to the house,
      But they never looked at us.
Their eyes were full of the mountain, lifting

Their measuring faces above our long hedge.
When they had gone I would climb the wall,
Looking for them among the thin sheep runs.
Their heads were a resolute darkness among ferns,
      They climbed with unsteady certainty.
I wondered what it was they knew the mountain had.

They would pass the last house, Lambert's, where
A violent gander, too old by many a Christmas,
Blared evil warning from his bitten moor,
Then it was open world, too high and clear
      For clouds even, where over heather
The free hare cleanly ran, and the summer sheep.

I knew this; and I knew all summer long
Those visionary gangs passed through our lanes,
Coming down at evening, their arms full
Of cowslips, moon daisies, whinberries, nuts,
         All fruits of the sliding seasons,
And the enormous experience of the mountain

That I who loved it did not understand.
In the summer, dust filled our winter ruts
With a level softness, and children walked
At evening through golden curtains scuffed
         From the road by their trailing feet.
They would drink tiredly at our wall, talking

Softly, leaning, their sleepy faces warm for home.
We would see them murmur slowly through our stiff
Gate, their shy heads gilded by the last sun.
One by one we would gather up the used jugs,
         The glasses. We would pour away
A little water. It would lie on the thick dust, gleaming.

Ransoms

(for Edward Thomas)

What the white ransoms did was to wipe away
The dry irritation of a journey half across
England. In the warm tiredness of dusk they lay
Like moonlight fallen clean onto the grass,

And I could not pass them. I wound
Down the window for them and for the still
Falling dark to come in as they would,
And then remembered that this was your hill,

Your precipitous beeches, your wild garlic.
I thought of you walking up from your house
And your heartbreaking garden, melancholy
Anger sending you into this kinder darkness,

And the shining ransoms bathing the path
With pure moonlight. I have my small despair
And would not want your sadness; your truth,
Your tragic honesty, are what I know you for.

I think of a low house upon a hill,
Its door closed now even to the hushing wind
The tall grass bends to, and all the while
The far-off salmon river without sound

Runs on below; but if this vision should
Be yours or mine I do not know. Pungent
And clean the smell of ransoms from the wood,
And I am refreshed. It was not my intent

12

To stop on a solitary road, the night colder,
Talking to a dead man, fifty years dead,
But as I flick the key, hear the engine purr,
Drive slowly down the hill, I'm comforted.

The white, star-shaped flowers of the Wood Garlic, *Allium ursinum Liliaceae,* are usually known as 'Ramsons'; but W. Keble Martin, in The Concise British Flora in Colour, (Ebury Press and Michael Joseph, 1965), calls them *Ransoms.* They grow profusely from April to June in the beech hangers above Edward Thomas's house outside Petersfield. Obviously, in the context of the poem, *Ransoms* means much more than the usual name.

Now the house sleeps among its trees,
Those charcoal scratches on the sky's
Good morning, and I walk the lane
That all night long has quietly gone
Down the cold hill, and quietly up
Until it reached that darkened top
Where the shrill light of a short day
Begins again the frozen glow

Of winter dawn. I contemplate
The wealth of day that has to wait
The recognition of my eye.
Reality is what we see,
Or what my senses all achieve;
What they believe, so I believe.
Around, the ring of hills wears light
Of morning like a steel helmet

And below them, in the brown
Cleansing of its floods, runs down
The brawling river. Now the owl,
That all night held its floating call
Over the terrified hedges, climbs
In clumsy blindness to the elm's
Black safety, there flops down,
A comfortable, daylight clown;

And little animals of night
Retire as silent as the light
To sleeping darkness. Closing the door,
I leave the white fields desert for
The loss of my descriptive eye.
The sunlit measures of the day
Are unregarded. I cut bread,
Knowing the world untenanted.

14

And yet, although my sight must stop
At the solid wall, a world builds up,
Feature by feature, root by root,
The soft advance of fields, daylight
Reaching west in the turn of life,
Personal, created world, half
Ignorant, half understood. And I
Complete from faulty memory

And partial complexities of sense
Those images of experience
That make approximate rivers move
Through the wrong world in which I live,
Or chart a neat uncertainty
Down major roads to Nowhere City;
But at the edge of what I know
The massed, appalling forests grow.

Through the long night the rough trucks grind
The highways, gears ripping blind,
Headlights awash on the tarmac;
All night long metallic traffic,
Racks of concrete, rams of girders,
Heavy oppression of cities
Forced by a crude growling. Yet all
Are Plato's shadows on the wall,

Noises drifting among shadows,
Shadows dying among echoes,
While clear eternities of light
Shine somewhere on the perfect world
We cannot know. My shadowed field
Lies in its flawed morning, and dirt
Falls in the slow ditches. Sunrise,
And the house wakes among its trees.

Postcards from Wales

Whenever I think of Wales, I hear the voices
Of children calling, and the world shrinks to the span
Of a dozen hills. As I wander to sleep
The water voices of the streams begin.

> *Green air, the truthful winds shall sing you*
> *Over the lean hill and the melancholy*
> *Valley of childhood.*

We swam free rivers that our tongues resembled,
We lit the summer dark with lazy fire
At the waterside. And when silence fell
It was not passing time we grew to hear,

> *Winter. The blind lake turns its solid*
> *Eye to the snowcloud. In the village*
> *The doors are fast, the chimneys fat with coalsmoke*

But the world changing, the tall hills tumbling,
The universe of terraces waning small.
Beyond brief rivers we heard the urgent sea
Knock to come in. It was a miracle

> *The spent salmon drops tail first to the sea.*
> *His lank sides heave. His exhausted eye*
> *Turns away for another year.*

Of our own discovering. Whenever I think of Wales,
I think of my leaving, the farewell valleys letting go
And the quick voices falling far behind in the dust
Off the dry tips. And I think of returning, too,

> *Cae Gwair is spotted with orchises;*
> *The earth, finding its own rich heat,*
> *Releases it in little purple columns.*

On some afternoon warm and loving, to a handful
Of fields by Teifi river and a cottage blind
With waiting. I know those rough, wind-turning
Walls were made in childhood, I know my mind

> *In September the cold ponies*
> *Return from the high moor. They kick*
> *Down the tottering stones and relish the gardens.*

Invents the long, immaculate weather of a year
Unpredictable as truth. But the river's voice
Is forever filling the valley, filling it,
And remembered voices are underneath my windows

Early Frost

We were warned about frost, yet all day the summer
Has wavered its heat above the empty stubble. Late
Bees hung their blunt weight,
Plump drops between those simplest wings, their leisure
An ignorance of frost.
My mind is full of the images of summer
And a liquid curlew calls from alps of air;

But the frost has come. Already under trees
Pockets of summer are dying, wide paths
Of the cold glow clean through the stricken thickets
And again I feel on my cheek the cut of winters
Dead. Once I awoke in a dark beyond moths
To a world still with freezing,
Hearing my father go to the yard for his ponies,

His hands full of frostnails to point their sliding
To a safe haul. I went to school,
Socks pulled over shoes for the streets' clear glass,
The early shops cautious, the tall
Classroom windows engraved by winter's chisel,
Fern, feather and flower that would not let the pale
Day through. We wrote in a cold fever for the morning

Play. Then boys in the exulting yard, ringing
Boots hard on winter, slapped with their polishing
Caps the arrows of their gliding, in steaming lines
Ran till they launched one by one
On the skills of ice their frail balance,
Sliding through life with not a fall in mind,
Their voices crying freely through such shouting

As the cold divided. I slid in the depth
Of the season till the swung bell sang us in.
Now insidious frost, its parched grains rubbing
At crannies, moved on our skin.
Our fingers died. Not the warmth
Of all my eight wide summers could keep me smiling.
The circle of the popping stove fell still
And we were early sped through the hurrying dark.

I ran through the bitterness on legs
That might have been brittle, my breath
Solid, grasping at stabs of bleak
Pain to gasp on. Winter branched in me, ice cracked
In my bleeding. When I fell through the teeth
Of the cold at my haven door I could not see

For locked tears, I could not feel the spent
Plenty of flames banked at the range,
Nor my father's hands as they roughed the blue
Of my knees. But I knew what he meant
With the love of his rueful laugh, and my true
World unfroze in a flood of happy crying,
As hot on my cheek as the sting of this present

Frost. I have stood too long in the orderly
Cold of the garden. I would not have again the death
Of that day come unasked as the comfortless dusk
Past the stakes of my fences. Yet these are my
Ghosts, they do not need to ask
For housing when the early frost comes down.
I take them in, all, to the settled warmth.

Stones

On the flat of the earth lie
Stones, their eyes turned
To earth's centre, always.
If you throw them they fly
Grudgingly, measuring your arm's
Weak curve before homing
To a place they know.

Digging, we may jostle
Stones with our thin tines
Into stumbling activity.
Small ones move most.
When we turn from them
They grumble to a still place.
It can take a month to grate

That one inch. Watch how stones
Clutter together on hills
And beaches, settling heavily
In unremarkable patterns.
A single stone can vanish
In a black night, making
Someone bury it in water.

We can polish some;
Onyx, perhaps, chalcedony,
Jasper and quartzite from
The edges of hard land.
But we do not alter them.
Once in a million years
Their stone hearts lurch.

Merman

(for Kit Barker)

When I first came to the air I fell
Through its empty thickets. Dry
Land attacked me, and I lay
With my skin in grit, drily.
The drab, sudden weight of my
Gagging flesh dragged me, would pull

Me down. Nor would my swimming
Bones erect me. It was a grunting
Crawl I moved at. There was not need
For the rough cords they locked me in.
Later, in the animal compound, pooled
In a small dead water of their making,

I hid my staring sex, and wept.
As my stale gills crumbled
Like bread, and slow lungs held
Air with a regular comfort,
I learned to prod locked bones
To a jolt of walking. Their sounds

Came last to my mouth
And were useful for freedom.
I who had been a sad monster
In the kept zoo of their fear
Live at equal liberty with
Them now. At dark I come

From watching the tame harbour
Where nudged ships depart,
And in my tideless cell I dream
The great seas break far over me,
Silent; and I dream I drift
In upright seagrowth, in the living water.

A Girl's Song

Early one morning
As I went out walking
I saw the young sailor
Go fresh through the fields.
His eye was as blue as
The sky up above us
And clean was his skin
As the colour of shells.

O where are you going,
Young sailor, so early?
And may I come with you
A step as you go?
He looked with his eye
And I saw the deep sea-tombs,
He opened his mouth
And I heard the sea roar.

And limp on his head
Lay his hair green as sea-grass
And scrubbed were his bones
By the inching of sand.
The long tides enfolded
The lines of his body
And slow corals grow
At the stretch of his hand.

I look from my window
In the first light of morning
And I look from my door
At the dark of the day,
But all that I see are
The fields flat and empty
And the black road run down
To Cardigan town.

Fishing the Teifi

Left bank and right,
I've fished this water since first light,
Pitching my early spinners
Into the river's mirrors,
Feeling the hook sink
Minutely, then I'd check, and bring it to the bank.

It was enough at first
To know the thrown perfection of each cast,
My eight-foot, fibreglass flinger
Growing from my hand, a finger
To set exactly down
My teal and black, mallard and claret, or coachman.

But I've had nothing on
All morning nor the longer afternoon.
For all his hunched attention
The empty heron's flown,
And now the soft-whistling otter
Glides his long belly into the blackening water.

From the bleak dark the hiss
Of a harsh wind turns my face
Down like a sheet, telling me to go.
But sleep tonight I know
Will not shut out this river, nor the gleam
Of big fish, sliding up to hook onto my dream.

The One Leaf

An oak leaf fell from the tree
Into my hand almost, so I kept it.
First in my fingers, very carefully,
Because it was mine. I wiped it,
Put it on my desk, near the typewriter.
Last autumn there were oak leaves falling everywhere.

I could have chosen from so many.
It lay there months, turning browner,
Before I no longer saw it. Now
Here it is again, an old letter
From plenty. From where I stand
This is the one leaf, in the cold house, on the cold ground.

It's Somebody's Birthday

This birthday man
Rises from my hot bed
Into his mirror.
When I groan
Out of his crumpled head
He prods my dewlap with a jeering finger.

Behind his eyes
Lie the slim silver boys
Called by my name.
No blind surprise
Nor moving without noise
Shall ever startle them inside that frame.

To my round skin
He will remain flat true,
Warning for warning.
I pull my stomach in,
March a hard step or two,
Shut loud the bathroom door, murder his morning.

Drummer Evans

There was a great elm in Drummer Evans's garden.
Half of his house it kept in daylight shadow; all summer
A chaffinch sang in its highest branches, swinging
In an invisible cage its music was so local.
Drummer dribbled it crumbs from his fingers
As he sat on a log, his back to the elm trunk,
One slow leg straight before him, and his yellow hand,
His fingers, playing intricate patterns on his other knee.
He was small, his eyes looked upward always.
His face was mild and ivory, composed and smooth.
He wore a black suit and a very wide hat and he called
All women Mrs. Jones, because it was easier.
I went to him Tuesdays and Saturdays for lessons.

My kettle-drum set on its three-legged stand,
He would flick its resonance with a finger and say,
"Now boy, two with each hand, away you go; and
Don't let the drumstick tamp." Tamp was a word for bounce,
We always used it. Away I'd go, two with each hand,
Back of the wrists to the skin, sticks held lightly,
And clumsily double beat with each hack fist,
Tap-tap, tap-tap, tap-tap, until that unskilled knock
Snarled in my tired arms and stuttered out.
I don't remember getting any better, but he'd nod,
Still for a while his drumming hand, and smile,
And say, "Again."
　　　　　　When I could play no more he'd take the sticks
And give to my stubborn drum a pliant eloquence.
I'd leave then. The bird was nearly always singing.
It never rained in Drummer Evan's garden.

Because I knew that I would never make
On an echoing hull those perfect measures
Heard in my head as I marched at the head of armies

Or rattling between the beat of my running heels,
I left the Drummer.

                              It was an idle sun
Recalled his garden, and an unclaimed bird
Singing from a thorn his tame bird's song
That brought the old man back,
Martial hands parading and muttering.
I went by the river's edge and stone bridge
To his thundering cottage.

For the air for half a mile was rhythmical thunder.
Roll after roll of exact, reverberant challenge,
The flamen of history unfurled their names from my books,
Agincourt, Malplaquet, Waterloo, Corunna,
And I reached at a gasp the Drummer's beleaguered garden.

Ringed by standing friends at the rim of his anger,
He stood strapped for war from the fury of their kindness,
Striking his sharp refusal of all pity
The women offered. "Come on," they called,
                              "Ah, come on Mr. Evans."
But he swept them away with the glory of his drumfire,
Hands flying high in volleys of retaliation.
The tree held its sunlight like a flag of honour
And helpless, uniformed men spoke out to him softly;
But his side-drum returned defiance for this old man
Whose proud skill told us he was Drummer Evans,
No common mister to be hauled to the Poorhouse.

Winter Song

Over the bluff hills
At the day's end
The diffident snow
Swirls before dropping

Blow wind, blow
That we may see
Your smooth body

The humble snow
Is waiting for darkness
So its soft light
Can muffle the hills

Blow wind, blow
The copse will be silent
The black trees empty

At the day's end
The small snow is scurrying
White bees in the moon
And the flying wind

Blow wind
Over the cold hills
For the moon is voiceless

Grass

I walk on grass more often
Than most men. Something in me
Still values wealth as a wide field
With blades locked close enough
To keep soil out of mind. It is a test
Of grass when I push a foot
Hard on its green spring. The high pastures
I mean, open to the unfenced wind,
Bitten by sheep.

      Go into Hereford,
My grandfather said, (his dwarf
Grass was scarce as emeralds,
The wet peat crept brown into his happiness),
In Hereford the grass is up to your waist.
We could not gather such unthinkable richness,
We stared over the scraped hill to luscious England.

Behind us the spun brook whitened
On boulders, and rolled, a slow thread
On the eyes, to bubbling pebbles.

I have been in wet grass up to the waist,
In loaded summer, on heavy summer mornings,
And when I came away my clothes, my shoes,
My hair even, were full of hard seeds
Of abundant grass. Brushes would not remove them.

Winters, I know grass is alive
In quiet ditches, in moist, secret places
Warmed by the two-hour sun. And as the year
Turns gently for more light,
Viridian grass moves out to lie in circles,
Live wreaths for the dying winter.

29

Soon roots of couch-grass,
Sly, white, exploratory, will lie
Bare to my spade. Smooth and pliable,
Their sleek heads harder
And more durable than granite.
It is worth fighting against grass.

Two Men

1. Billy Price

He would open the loft early
And his soft-voiced flock
Turned in the morning
Like a bird with a hundred wings.

On workless days he would sing
Freely, and girls in neighbouring
Backyards applauded him
With joined choruses and the frankness of their smiles.

At evening he would signal in his pigeons.
When I began to whistle I learned this call;
A ladder of falling notes across the bars as the birds
Folded themselves home.

2. John Williams

His father had drunk away many acres
And a whole flock of mountain sheep.
He had been tall, red-bearded, strong as legend,
Ridden to market on a pony much too small,

But John Williams was deliberately not like this.
Mild and silver from his youth,
He had refused even to grow very much.
At fourteen I was inches over his eighty years.

The day he was eighty we leaned on his gate
And he told me of his fading eyes.
There was a signpost on the horizon opposite
He could scarcely see. Staring at that far

Mountain-edge, I could see only the dissolving
Motes of the air. But he had turned away.
"When you are old," he said, "when you are old
You know where all the fingerposts are."

Dog

On a field like a green roof
Pitched by the sea wind
A patch of uncertain sheep
Each poised on pointed hoof
Ready for running
Stare at the coiled bitch
Alert for their turning

And stamp as she sidles
And freezes. They pick
At the steep field, they back,
Disturbing the nervous edge
Of their fleecy circle.
Slowly the bitch inches
And with a rush

Channels the stunned run.
They stream in a prim file
Through the one marked gap
In the leaning hedge,
And Fan, tongue sideways lolling,
Ushers them softly through.
Adrift on the stiff hill

The cold shepherd does not even watch them.

Space Miner

(for Robert Morgan)

His face was a map of traces where veins
Had exploded bleeding in atmospheres too
Frail to hold that life, and scar tissue
Hung soft as pads where his cheekbones shone
Under the skin when he was young.
He had worked deep seams where encrusted ore,
Too tight for his diamond drill, had ripped
Strips from his flesh. Dust from a thousand metals
Silted his lungs and softened the strength
Of his muscles. He had worked the treasuries
Of many near stars, but now he stood on the moving
Pavement reserved for cripples who had served well.
The joints of his hands were dry and useless
Under the cold gloves issued by the government.

Before they brought his sleep in a little capsule
He would look through the hospital window
At the ships of young men bursting into space.
For this to happen he had worked till his body broke.
Now they flew to the farthest worlds in the universe;
Mars, Eldorado, Mercury, Earth, Saturn.

The Dead

(after the Welsh of Gwenallt, 1899-1969)

Reaching fifty, a man has time to recognise
His ordinary humanity, the common echoes
In his own voice. And I think with compassion
Of the graves of friends who died. When I was young,

Riding the summer on a bike from the scrap-yard,
Kicking Wales to victory with all I could afford —
A pig's bladder — how could I have known
That two of my friends would suffer the torn

Agony of slimy death from a rotten lung,
Red spittle letting their weakening
Living into a bucket? They were our neighbours,
Lived next door. We called them the Martyrs

Because they came from Merthyr Tydfil, that
Town of furnaces. Whenever I thought
I'd laugh, a cough ripped over the wall,
Scraping my ribs with cinders. It was all

Done at last, and I crept in to look,
Over the coffin's edge and the black
Rim of the Bible, at the dry flesh free
Of breath, too young for the cemetery.

And I protest at such death without dignity,
Death brutally invoked, death from the factory,
Immature death, blind death, death which mourning
Does not comfort, without tears. I bring

From my mind a small house huge with death,
Where heavy women cut sticks, deal with
The fires, the laborious garden, their little
Money dissolving in the hand. Terrible

Are the blasphemous wars and savageries I
Have lived through, animal cruelty
Loose like a flame through the whole world;
Yet here on Flower Sunday, in a soiled

Acre of graves, I lay down my gasping roses
And lilies pale as ice as one who knows
Nothing certain, nothing; unless it is
My own small place and people, agony and sacrifice.

Owls

The owls are flying. From hedge to hedge
Their deep-mouthed voices call the fields
Of England, stretching north and north,
To a sibilant hunt above ditches;
And small crawlers, bent in crevices, yield
Juice of their threaded veins, with

A small kernel of bones. It was earlier
I walked the lace of the sea at this south
Edge, walked froths of the fallen moon
Bare-legged in the autumn water
So cold it set my feet like stones
In its inches, and I feel on breath

And ankles the touch of the charged sea
Since. I saw in my lifting eyes the flat
Of this one country, north stretching,
And north. I saw its hills, the public light
Of its cities, and every blatant tree
Burning, with assembled autumn burning.

I know the same sun, in a turn
Of earth, will bring morning, grey
As gulls or mice to us. And I know
In my troubled night the owls fly
Over us, wings wide as England,
And their voices will never go away.

October in the Lane

October in the lane, and the thin harebells,
Ghosts of their deep Augusts, pine in the hedges.
Puffed leaves thicken the crawling ditches
And tired wasps labour in the air,

Heavy with dying. Our trees prepare
The black calligraphies of winter, we strip
Our fields for the frost fire. Now roses drop
From the wall their falls of petals

And cheat my eyes with snowflakes. Smells
Of marauding weather come coldly in with the dark.
I remember a spring of snow that fell without mark
On my head and white hurry as I thudded for home

And we laughed to see how soon I became,
In a falling minute, a seven year old, white-haired man.
In the kitchen mirror I watched the quick years run
From the warm, and I wiped from my head

The unready white my April time pretended.
So many weathers have spread their tempers near me
That empty winters stretch behind my mirror
And the keenest razor will not shift their snowfalls.

A True Death

(for Vernon Watkins 1906-1967)

When summer is dead, when evening
October is dying, the pendulum
Heart falters, and the firm
Blood hangs its drops in a swing
Of stone. Laughing, we catch breath
Again. But his was the true death

Our rehearsals imitate. I lived
On the charred hills where industrial
Fires for a hundred years had grieved
All things growing. On still,
On the stillest days, a burnish
Of sea glinted at the world's edge

And died with the sun. There
Were twenty miles of Wales between
My streams and the water lore
He knew. He watched the green
Passages of the sea, how it rides
The changing, unchanging roads

Of its hollowing power. Caves
From his flooded cliffs called to him,
Dunes with their harsh grasses
Sang, the river-mouths spoke of home
In Carmarthen hills. Small stones
Rang like bells, touching his hands.

Last year we sat in his garden,
Quietly, in new wooden chairs,
Grasshoppers rasped on the hot lawn.
Shadows gathered at his shoulders
As he spoke of the little tormentil,
Tenacious flower; growing there still.

38

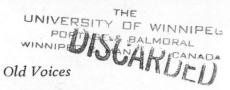

Old Voices

First the one bell, heavy, behind it
Centuries of controlled certainty, swung
With an enormous sound past
The kneeling city; it is the first
Heard stone in an architecture of ringing.
And sung in at built intervals, at
The joint of locked structure, the voice
Of the second bell. The foundation is

Set on unimpeded air. An age
Of cut stone and iron — those old
Technologies — has its immense medieval
Tongues bellowing again. Now all
The small bells filigree and stretch
A long nave in the ear and a pulled
Spire of sailing clamour. Resonant
Cathedrals of listening are launched

On the open day. But bells are not
Peaceful; are arrogant with the complete
World of their origin. Think, imagine,
In the clack of swords they began,
Short on their own shields the flat beat
Struck, so that erratic courage set
Hard in the metal; then the high edge,
Turning in the urgency of the charge,

Rang through the heads of wives
At their keen mourning. Hacking the bent
Angles of helmets, rough blades cracked again
The wombs that bore these splintered heads
In their early down. From such sounds,
From the held quiet after, the brazen
Complexities of the loud tower grew.
There was time for the patterns of victory,

39

And space on the fat plains of grain
For building of flawless bells. The lost
In their slate hills had tongues only,
Grew old in the slow labour
Of changing myths. Through the mist
Of altering voices their stories spun,
Through generations of telling. Spiral
Images from the belfries, the metal

Confections of chiming, are not
For the mountains. Old men tell
Of an impermanent peace, a fragile
Faith is passed through narrative
Villages in syllables of live
Whispers. Foolish now to regret
Centuries of locked exile. It happened.
We have heads full of easy legend

And elegies like the cold sun
Of treeless autumn. I carry
Such tunes in my head like the thin
Silence the bells hang in. But from
These reaching fields my surnamed
Fathers came, the great cathedrals
Counted them. I walk their lanes,
My shoes cover the concave stones

Worn by their slow tolling.
If I speak with the quick brooks
Of the permanent hills, in my saying
See hordes of the dark tribes stand,
Their faces hidden, my hand
In its perfect glove of skin holds
Other ghosts. We step the streets
Uneasily, disturbed by bells.